Easy Peasy Thai!

Your Thai Phrase Book To Go!

by

Areva Champan

Table of Contents

History and Introduction

Thailand's national and official language is Thai, formerly known as Siamese. It is the native language of the majority of the population and is closely linked to languages of neighboring countries such as Laos, Vietnam and Burma. Thai script is related to the Khmer writing system.

The origin of the language remains a topic of much academic debate. It may have come from either the Tai-Kadai language family or the Austro-Asiatic languages both prevalent in South East Asia. The Royal Institute of Thailand (RIT) is the governing body of the Thai language. It published the first Royal Institute Dictionary in 1950 and updates the dictionary as necessary, with several publications having been produced since.

The four major regional dialects of spoken Thai are Phasa Klang, Phasa Nuea, Phasa Lao and Phasa Tai. Phasa Klang is spoken in the central region and around Bangkok, Phasa Lao is spoken in the north-eastern part of Thailand (which makes up much of the farming community) and Phasa Nuea is spoken around the northern areas of Thailand. Phasa Klang (or Central Thai) is the dialect traditionally used by the educated classes in Bangkok. It is the language of business, the media, public announcements, is also used in the government and is taught in schools and universities. Even though people from different parts of the country may speak with different dialects, each with a varying vocabulary, speakers of the various dialects all understand Phasa Klang.

Thai speakers tend to change their language depending on the social context. When writing or talking to strangers, Thai can be very formal. Many polite terms are used to address people and polite participles are added to sentences to convey respect. When addressing the royal family, Thai speakers make use of language suitable for the royal court. When speaking to monks or discussing Buddhism, the language changes to suit religious matters. For everyday Thai, used between friends and family, an informal version is used. Everyday Thai does not require all the extra polite terms of address and may contain a lot of slang.

Pronunciation and Grammar

Thai is a language which makes use of different tones to give
meaning to its words - each syllable of a word can have a low, mid,
high, rising or falling tone and the tone with which you pronounce a
word will determine its meaning: '*mee*', for instance, pronounced
with a rising tone translates to '*a bear*', '*mee*' pronounced with a
mid-tone translates to '*has*' and '*mee*' pronounced with a falling tone
is '*egg noodles*'. For this reason a beginning learner of Thai who is
not accustomed to using tones might find it hard to get a message
across, although the context within which a word is used often helps
the listener understand it!

Thai words do not change their forms to indicate the subjects,
plurals, tenses, or possession as is found in English. Words which
depict these meanings in themselves are often added to sentences to
convey such meanings: "*Jack go home yesterday*". Adjectives,
adverbs and other modifiers are usually placed after the words which
they modify ("*house big*", "*Jack go quickly*"), without any linking
verbs between them ("*Jack excited*") and articles (a, the) are not used
at all.

Thai has forty-four consonants and thirty two vowel sounds
(including short vowels, long vowels and diphthongs). Many of the
consonants have a very close, or often the same sound, but will differ
in how they affect the tone of the syllable in which they are found.
The sound of a consonant will vary depending on where it is placed
in a word: consonants at the end of a word or syllable are unvoiced
or not pronounced completely (they are 'stopped' inside the mouth
before they make a sound – an English word pair such as *cab* and
cap would therefore be pronounced the same: '*cap*', without the
release of breath of the '*p*' sound).

The standard polite means of address for both men and women is to
use the pronoun "*chan*" to refer to oneself, though men commonly
use "*pom*" instead. A politeness particle can and should be added to
the end of any sentence to convey one's politeness; women use
"*kha*" and men use "*khrap*".

Vowels

Latin / Thai		English Sound
a / อะ , อั_		"**u**" as in "**sun**"
a / อา		"**a**" as in "**father**"
ae / แอ		"**a**" as in "**dad**" (long "**a**" sound)
ae / แอะ		"**a**" as in "**at**" (short "**a**" sound)
e / เอะ		"**e**" as in "**very**"
e / เอ		"**e**" as in "**very**", but with a longer "**e**" sound
er / เออะ		"**e**" as in "**writer**"
er / เออ		"**e**" as in "**writer**", but with a longer "**e**" sound
i / อี		"**ee**" as in "**keen**"
i / อิ		"**y**" as in "**happy**"

o / เอาะ		"o" as in "**often**"
o / โอะ		"o" as in "**dot**"
o / โอ		"o" as in "**dot**", but with a longer "o" sound
o / อ		"**aw**" as in "**law**"
u / อึ		"**oo**" as in "**book**", but with relaxed, non-rounded lips (short sound)
u / อื		"**oo**" as in "**soon**", but with relaxed, non-rounded lips (long sound)
u / อุ		"**oo**" as in "**book**" (short "**oo**" sound)
u / อู		"**oo**" as in "**soon**" (long "**oo**" sound)

Consonants

Latin / Thai		English Sound
* / อ		silent as a consonant – it simply carries the vowel.
b / บ		"b" as in "**bucket**", or "**p**" as in "**cup**" at the end of a word/syllable.
bp / ป		"b" as in "**bucket**", but pronounced slightly more towards a "**p**"; a combination of a "**b**" and a "**p**" sound.
ch/t / ฉ , ช , ฌ		"ch" as in "**chicken**", or "**t**" as in "cat" at the end of a word/syllable.
d / ด , ฎ		"d" as in "**dog**" ", or "**t**" as in "**cat**" at the end of a word/syllable.
dt / ต , ฏ		"t" as in "**tortoise**", but pronounced slightly heavier – a combination of a "**d**" and a "**t**" sound.
f/ph / ฝ , ฟ		"f" as in "**fairy**", or "**p**" as in "**cup**" at the end of a word/syllable.
g/k / ก		"g" as in "**great**", or "**k**" as in "**kind**" at the end of a word.
h / ห		"h" as in "house", but sometimes silent.
h / ฮ		"h" as in "**house**"

j/t / จ		"**j**" as in "**joy**", or "**t**" as in "**cat**" at the end of a word/syllable.
kh / ข , ฃ , ค , ฅ , ฆ		"**k**" as in "**kind**"
l / ล , ฬ		as in "**l**" "**lovely**"
lea / ฦ		"**li-**" as in " **learn**"
lea / ฦา		"**lea-**" as in "**learn**", but with a longer vowel sound
m / ม		"**m**" as in "**mother**"
n / น , ณ		"**n**" as in "**nest**"
ng / ง		"**ng**" as in "**sing**"
ph / พ , ผ , ภ		"**p**" as in "**plant**"
r / ร		"**r**" as in "**riddle**", but with more friction, or "**n**" as in "**noodle**" at the end of a word/syllable.
ru/ri / ฤ		"**roo-**" as in "**brook**" (short "**oo**" sound) / "**ri-**" as in "**rid**"
ru/ri / ฤา		"**roo-**" as in "**brood**" (long "**oo**" sound) / "**ree-**" as in "**reed**"
s / ศ , ษ , ส , ซ		"**s**" as in "**star**", or "**t**" as in "cat" at the end of a word/syllable.

th / ฐ , ฑ , ฒ , ถ , ท, ธ		"**t**" as in "**tortoise**"
w / ว		"**w**" as in "**wing**"
y / ย		"**y**" as in "**yard**"
y/n / ญ		"**y**" as in "**yard**", or "**n**" as in "**bun**" at the end of a word/syllable.

Digraphs

Latin / Thai		English Sound
a/am/an รร		"**u**" as in "**sum**" in a central position (closed), "**un**" as in "**sun**" in a final position (open).
j / จร		"**j**" as in "**joy**"
s/t ทร , ศร		"**s**" as in "**star**"

Diphthongs

Latin / Thai		English Sound
ai / ไอ , ใอ		As the pronoun, "**I**", or as "**ie**" in "**pie**"
ao / เอา		As "**ou**" in "**out**"
ua / อัวะ (open) **/** อัว (closed)		As "**ua**" in **equal**"
eua / เอือะ (open) / เอือ (closed)		As "**ua**" in **equal**", but with relaxed, non-rounded lips.
ia / เอียะ (open) **/** เอีย (closed)		"**ia**" as in "**Virginia**"

Everyday Phrases

	Translation	How to say it
Hello.	sawat di krap / ka สวัสดี ครับ / ค่ะ	sa what dee crup / ka
Good morning.	sawat di don chao สวัสดีตอนเช้า	sa what dee don chow
Good day.	sawat di krap / ka สวัสดี ครับ / ค่ะ	sa what dee crup / ka
Good evening.	sawat di don yen สวัสดีตอนเย็น	sa what dee don yen
Good night.	non lap fan di นอนหลับฝันดี	non lup fun dee
Hi.	sawat di สวัสดี	sa what dee
Goodbye.	la gon, pai gon na ลาก่อน, ไปก่อนนะ	la gone , pie gone na
Nice to meet you.	yin di ti dai rujak ยินดีที่ได้รู้จัก	yin dee tee die roo juck
How are you?	sabai di mai สบายดีไหม	sa bye dee my
Fine, thank you.	sabai di khob khun สบายดี ขอบคุณ	sa bye dee cop coon
What is your name?	khun chue arai คุณชื่ออะไร	coon chew a rye

My name is.	chan chue … ฉัน ชื่อ …	chun chew … ("**chun**" rhymes with "**one**")
Yes.	khrap / kha ครับ / ค่ะ	crup / ka
No.	mai ไม่	my
Please.	garuna กรุณา	garoona
Thank you.	khop khun khrap / kha ขอบคุณ ครับ / ค่ะ	cop coon crup / ka
You are welcome.	mai pen rai ไม่เป็นไร	my pen rye
Please, can you help me?	garuna chuai chan dai mai khrap / kha กรุณาช่วยฉันได้ไหม ครับ / ค่ะ	garoona choy chun die my crup / ka
Excuse me.	kho tot khrap / ka ขอโทษ ครับ / ค่ะ	caw tot crup / ka ("**caw**" sounds like "**core**" without the "**r**")
Pardon me.	kho apai ขออภัย	caw a pie
I am sorry	chan sia jaiฉัน เสียใจ	chun sia jie ("**sia**" sounds like "**seer**" without the "**r**", ("**jie**" sounds like "**jive**" without the "**ve**")
Do you speak English?	khun phut phasa angrit dai maiคุณพูดภาษาอังกฤษได้ไหม	coon poot passa ungreet die my

Is there someone here who speaks English?	ti ni mi krai tip hut pasa angrit dai mai ที่นี่มีใครที่พูดภาษาอังกฤษได้ไหม	Tee nee mee cry tee poot passa ungreet die my
Please repeat that!	garuna phut ik ti di mai khrap / kha กรุณาพูดอีกทีได้ไหม ครับ / ค่ะ	garoona poot eek tee die my crup / ka
I understand.	chan khao jai ฉันเข้าใจ	chun cow jie
I do not understand.	chan mai khao jai ฉัน ไม่เข้าใจ	chun my cow jie
What does it mean?	man mai kwam wa yang ngai มันหมายความว่ายังไง	mun my kwam wa young ngai
What time is it?	donni gi mong ตอนนี้กี่โมง	donnee key mong
Where is the bathroom?	hongnam yu nai ห้องน้ำอยู่ไหน	hong num you nai ("nai" sounds the same as "nigh")
Where can I find a telephone?	chan samart ha torasap ti nai ฉันสามารถหาโทรศัพท์ที่ไหน	chun sa-mart ha torasup tee nai

Accommodation

	Translation	How to say it
Do you have any rooms available?	mi hong wang mai มีห้องว่างไหม	me hong wung my ("**wung**" rhymes with "**sung**")
How much is a room for one person?	hong diao tao rai ห้องเดียวเท่าไร	hong dee-oh tao rye
How much is a room for two people?	hong khu tao rai ห้องคู่เท่าไร	hong coo tao rye
May I see the room first?	kho du hong gon dai mai ขอดูห้องก่อนได้ไหม	caw doo hong gone die my
Does the room come with...	nai hong mi ... mai ในห้องมี ... ไหม	nai hong me ... my
... a bathroom?	hong nam ห้องน้ำ	hong num ("**num**" as in "**number**")
... a telephone?	torasap โทรศัพท์	torasup
... bedsheets?	pa pu ti non ผ้าปูที่นอน	pa poo tee non
... pillows?	mon หมอน	mon

… towels?	pa chet dtua ผ้าเช็ดตัว	pa chet tour ("**tour**" as in the English word, but without an "**r**" sound)
… shower?	fak bua ฝักบัว	fug boo-ah ("**fug**" rhymes with English "**mug**")
… a TV?	toratat โทรทัศน์	tore a tut
Do you have anything...	mi arai มีอะไร.....	me a rye …
… bigger?	yai gwa ใหญ่กว่า	yai ("**yai**" rhymes with "**high**") gua ("**gua**" as in "**guava**")
… cleaner?	sa-at kwa สะอาดกว่า	sa art gua
… smaller?	lek kwa เล็กกว่า	lek ("**leg**", but with a "**k**" ending") gua
… cheaper?	tuk twa ถูกกว่า	took gua
… quieter?	ngiap kwa เงียบกว่า	ngee-up ("**ng**" as in "**sing**") gua
… better?	di kwa ดีกว่า	dee gua

Do you offer...	mi borigan … mai มีบริการ … ไหม	me boree-gun … my
... a safe?	dtu sef ตู้เซฟ	too safe
... lockers?	dtu lokke ตู้ล็อคเกอร์	too locker
Is breakfast included?	ruam ahan chao mai khrap / kha รวมอาหารเช้าไหมครับ/ค่ะ	roo-um a-hun chow my crup / ka
Is supper included?	ruam ahan yen mai khrap / ka รวมอาหารเย็นไหมครับ/ค่ะ	roo-um a hun yen my crup / ka
When is breakfast?	ahan chao wela tao rai อาหารเช้าเวลาเท่าไหร่	a hun chow whe-la ("whe" as in "where") tao rye
When is supper?	ahan yen wela tao rai อาหารเย็นเวลาเท่าไหร่	a hun yen whe-la ("whe" as in "where") tao rye
Ok, I will take it.	oke chan ja ao an ni โอเค ฉันจะเอาอันนี้	okay, chun ja ou un nee. ("ja" as in "jar" ; "ou" as in "out")
I will stay for... night(s).	chan ja yu … khen ฉันจะอยู่....คืน	chan ja you … kern ("kern" as in "kernel")
Can you suggest other	khun samart nenam rongrem en dai mai khrap / ka	coon samart nay-num rong-

hotels?	คุณสามารถแนะนำโรงแรมอื่นได้ไหมครับ/ค่ะ	ram urn die my crup / ka
Please clean my room.	garuna tam kwam sa-at hong chan กรุณาทำความสะอาดห้องฉัน	garoona tum guam sa-art hong chun
Could you please wake me at...?	garuna bpluk chan dton wela … กรุณาปลุกฉันตอนเวลา.....	garoona plook chun don whe-la …
I would like to check out.	chan yak ja chek aot ฉันอยากจะขอเช็คเอาท์	chun yuck ja check out

Authorities

	Translation	How to say it
It was a misunderstanding	kaojai pit gan เข้าใจผิดกัน	cow jie peet gun
I haven't done anything wrong.	chan mai dai tam arai pit plat ฉันไม่ได้ทำอะไรผิดพลาด	chun my die tum a rye peet plart ("**plart**" rhymes with "**part**" without the "**r**" sound)
Am I under arrest?	chan don jam khuk mai ฉันโดนจำคุกไหม	chun don jum cook my ("**jum**" as in "**jump**")
Where are you taking me?	ja pa chan pai ti nai จะพาฉันไปที่ไหน	ja pa chun pie tee nai ("**pa**" as in "**party**")
I want to talk to a lawyer.	kho kui gap tanai kwam ขอคุยกับทนายความ	caw quee gup ton nai guam ("**quee**" as in "**queen**" ; "**ton**" as in the English word)
I am an American / British / Australian / Canadian citizen.	chan ke kon amerigan / angrit / ostrelia / kanada ฉันคือคน อเมริกัน / อังกฤษ / ออสเตรเรีย/ แคนนดา	chun cur con American / Ungreet / Australia / Canada
I want to talk to	chan yak ja kui gap satantut /	chun yuk ja

the American / British / Australian / Canadian embassy / consulate.	satan gongsun amerigan / angrit / ostrelia / kanada ฉันอยากจะคุยกับสถานทูต / สถานกงสุล อเมริกัน/อังกฤษ/ออสเตรเลีย/แคนนาดา	quee gup sa-tarn toot / sa-tarn gong-soon American / Ungreet / Australia / Canada
Can I just pay a fine now?	chan kho jai kha bprap donni dai mai ฉันขอจ่ายค่าปรับตอนนี้ได้ไหม	chan caw jie car prup don nee die my ("**car**" as in the English word, but without an "**r**" sound ; "**prup**" rhymes with "**pup**")

Bars, Restaurants and Food

	Translation	How to say it
I would like to make a reservation for tonight.	chan yak ja jong ti samrap ken ni ฉัน อยากจะจองที่สำหรับคืนนี้	chun yuck ja jong tee sum-rup kern nee ("**jong**" starts with the same sound as "**John**" and the ending rhymes with "**song**")
I would like to make a reservation for tomorrow night.	chan yak ja jong ti samrap ken prung ni ฉัน อยากจะจองที่สำหรับคืนพรุ่งนี้	chun yuck ja jong tee sum-rup kern proong nee.
I have a reservation.	chan jong lew khrap / kha ฉัน จองแล้วครับ/ค่ะ	chan jong lou crup / ka ("**lou**" as in "**loud**"
Can I have a table for two please?	kho ti samrap song khon khrap/kha ขอที่สำหรับสองคน ครับ/ค่ะ	caw tee sum-rup song con crup / ka
When is closing time?	pet gi mong khrap / kha ปิดกี่โมง ครับ/ค่ะ	pert gee mong crup / ka ("**pert**" as in "**expert**" ; "**gi**" as in "**gift**"
Do you know a good restaurant?	ru jak ran ahan ti di mai khrap / kha รู้จักร้านอาหารที่ดีไหม ครับ/ค่ะ	roo juck run a-hun tee dee my crup / ka

Do you serve alcohol?	ti ni mi elkohol mai ที่นี้มีแอลกอฮอล์ไหม	tee nee mee alcohol my
Can we please see the menu?	rao kho du menu dai mai เราขอดูเมนูได้ไหม	rou caw doo menu die my ("**rou**" as in "**round**")
Do you have a children's menu?	mi menu samrap dek mai มีเมนูสำหรับเด็กไหม	me menu sum-rup deck my
What is today's special?	wan ni mi arai piset วันนี้มีอะไรพิเศษ	one nee mee a rye pee set
Is there a house specialty?	ti ran ni mi arai piset doi chepo ที่ร้านนี้มีอะไรพิเศษโดยเฉพาะ	tee run nee mee a rye pee set doi chip-o ("**doi**" as in "**doink**" ; "**o**" as in "**ore**")
Is there a local specialty?	tew ni mi arai piset doi chepo แถวนี้มีอะไรพิเศษโดยเฉพาะ	tow ("**tow**" as in "**town**") nee mee a rye pee set doi chip-o
What do you recommend?	khun ja nenam arai di คุณจะแนะนำอะไรดี	coon ja nay-num a rye dee
Can I look in the kitchen?	kao pai du nai hong krua dai mai เข้าไปดูในห้องครัวได้ไหม	caw pie doo nai hong crew-a die my
A la carte	อาหารที่มีอยู่ในเมนูได้ตามใจชอบ ahan ti mi yu nai menu dai dtaam jai chop	a-hun tee mee you nai menu dai tum jie chop

Breakfast	ahan chao อาหารเช้า	a-hun chow
Lunch	ahan glang wan อาหารกลางวัน	a-hun glung one ("**glung**" rhymes with "**lung**")
Dinner	dinne ดินเนอร์	dinner
Supper	ahan yen อาหารเย็น	a-hun yen
Salt	gluea เกลือ	gluer (rhymes with "**bluer**", but without the "**r**" sound)
Pepper	prik thai พริกไทย	prick thai
Black pepper	prik thai dam พริกไทยดำ	prick thai dum
Butter	nui เนย	nooey (rhymes with "**gooey**", but without rounded lips)
Cream	krim ครีม	cream
Chicken	gai ไก่	guy
Fish	bpla ปลา	plug (without the "**g**" sound)
Ham	hem แฮม	ham
Beef	nuea เนื้อ	newer (without the rolling "**r**" sound)

Veal	nuea luk wua เนื้อลูกวัว	newe look woo-ha
Sausage	sai grok ไส้กรอก	si-grog ("si" as in "side")
Eggs	kai ไข่	kai (rhymes with "**sky**")
Cheese	chit ชีส	cheese
Salad	salat สลัด	salad
Vegetables	pak ผัก	puck
Fruit	ponlamai ผลไม้	pon-la-my
Fresh	sot สด	sot
Toast	kanom bpang bping ขนมปังปิ้ง	canom pang ping
Bread	kanom bpang ขนมปัง	canom pang
Sugar	nam dtan น้ำตาล	num tun
Rice	kaw ข้าว	cow
Noodles	bami บะหมี่	bar-me (without an "**r**" sound)
Pasta	pat dta พาสต้า	pasta
Beans	tua ถั่ว	tour (without an "**r**" sound)
Tea	nam cha น้ำชา	num char

		(without a rolling "**r**" sound)
Coffee	gafe กาแฟ	gar-fare (without rolling "**r**" sounds)
Milk	nom นม	nom
Juice	nam ponlamai น้ำผลไม้	num pon la my
Orange juice	nam som น้ำส้ม	num som
Lemon	manaw มะนาว	ma-now
Soft drink	soda โซดา	soda
Ice	nam keng น้ำแข็ง	num kang ("**kang**" as in "**kangaroo**")
Coke	kok โค้ก	coke
Water	nam น้ำ	num
Bubbly water	nam at lom น้ำอัดลม	num ut lom ("**ut**" as in "**but**" ; "**lom**" rhymes with "**bomb**")
Tonic water	nam tonik น้ำโทนิก	num tonic
Beer	bia เบียร์	beer
Wine	wai ไวน์	wine

White wine	wai kaw ไวน์ขาว	wine cow
Red wine	wai deng ไวน์แดง	wine dang
Whiskey	witki วิสกี้	whiskey
Rum	ram รัม	rum
Vodka	wodga วอดก้า	vodka
A bottle	kuat ขวด	coo-ut
I am a vegetarian.	chan bpen mangsawirat ฉันเป็นมังสะวิรัต	chun pen mung-sa-wee-rut
I don't eat meat.	chan mai kin nuea ฉันไม่กินเนื้อ	chun my keen newer (without the rolling "r" sound)
I don't eat pork.	chan mai kin mu ฉันไม่กินหมู	chun my keen moo
I want a dish containing...	chan yak ja dai ahan ti mi … ฉันอยากจะได้อาหารที่มี....	chun yuck ja die a-hun tee mee …
I only eat kosher food.	chan yak ja dai ahan ti samart gin dai dtaam gotmai yiw ฉันอยากจะได้อาหารที่สามารถกินได้ ตามกฎของยิว	chun yuck ja die a-hun tee samart geen die tum got-my yew ("geen" rhymes with "keen")
I'm allergic to...	chan pe ฉันแพ้...	chun pear (without the

		rolling "r" sound)
Waiter!	dek serp เด็กเสริฟ	deck serve
Waitress!	dek serp เด็กเสริฟ	deck serve
Excuse me, waiter? / Excuse me, waitress?	kho ropguan dek serp noi ขอรบกวนเด็กเสริฟหน่อย	caw rob-guin deck serve noy ("**guin**" as in "**penguin**" ; "**noy**" rhymes with "**boy**")
May I have a glass of...?	kho gaew neng ขอ...แก้วนึง	caw gow ner-ng ("**gow**" rhymes with "**cow**" ; "**ner**" as in "**nerd**", "**ng**" as in "**sing**"
May I have a cup of...?	kho … tui neng ขอ...ถ้วยนึง	caw toy ner-ng
May I have a bottle of...?	kho … kuat neng ขอ..ขวดนึง	caw quat ner-ng ("**quat**" as in "**quart**" without the "**r**" sound)
Can I have a fork?	kho som noi ขอส้อมหน่อย	caw som noy
Can I have a spoon?	kho chon noi ขอช้อนหน่อย	caw chon noy
Can I have a knife?	kho mit noi ขอมีดหน่อย	caw meet noy

Can I have a plate?	kho jan noi ขอจานหน่อย	caw jun noy ("**jun**" as in "**jungle**")
Can I have a glass?	kho gaew noi ขอแก้วหน่อย	caw gow noy
I am hungry.	chan hiw ฉันหิว	chun hew
I am thirsty.	chan hiw nam ฉันหิวน้ำ	chun hew num
I would like to order.	chan yak ja sang lew ฉันอยากจะสั่งแล้ว	chan yuck ja sung lou ("**lou**" as in "**loud**")
I would like a water.	chan yak ja sang nam ฉันอยากจะสั่งน้ำ	chun yuck ja sung num
I would like a coffee.	chan yak ja sang gafe ฉันอยากจะสั่งกาแฟ	chun yuck ja sung gar-fare (without rolling "**r**" sounds)
… with milk.	sai nom....ใส่นม	si-nom
I would like a tea.	chan yak ja sang nam cha ฉันอยากจะสั่งน้ำชา	chun yuck ja sung nam cha ("**cha**" as in "**char**" without the rolling "**r**" sound)
…. with lemon.	sai manaw ....ใส่มะนาว	si- ma-now
I would like an ice tea.	chan yak ja sang cha yen ฉันอยากจะสั่งชาเย็น	chun yuck ja sung cha yen
I would like a	chan yak ja sang nam at lom	chan yuck ja sung

soft drink.	ฉันอยากจะสั่งน้ำอัดลม	num ut-lom
I would like a bottle of wine.	chan yak ja sang wai kuat neng ฉันอยากจะสั่งไวน์ขวดนึง	chun yuck ja sung wine coo-ut ner-ng
Can you also bring us bread and butter?	khun bpai ao kanombpang gap nui dui dai mai คุณไปเอาขนมปังกับเนยด้วยได้ไหม	coon pie ou kanom pung gup nooey doy die my
What do you have for desserts?	ahan wan mi arai bang อาหารหวาน มีอะไรบ้าง	a-hun one mee a-rye bung ("**bung**" rhymes with "**sung**")
One more, please.	kho ik an neng ขออีกอันหนึ่ง	caw eek un ner-ng
Another round, please.	kho ik rop neng ขออีกรอบหนึ่ง	caw eek rob ner-ng
It was delicious.	man aroi di มันอร่อยดี	mun a-roy dee
Please clear the plates.	garuna gep jan กรุณาเก็บจาน	garoona gep jun ("**gep**" has the same "**g**" sound as "**get**")
Where is the bathroom?	hong nam yu ti nai ห้องน้ำอยู่ที่ไหน	hong num you tee nai
Please bring me the bill.	kho ao bin ma hai chan noi ขอเอาบิลมาให้ฉันหน่อย	caw ou been ma hi chun noy

Colors and Numbers

	Translation	How to say it
White	si kaw / สีขาว	see cow
Yellow	si lueang / สีเหลือง	see lue-ung ("**lue**" as in "**blue**" and "**ung**" as in "**sung**")
Orange	si som / สีส้ม	see som ("**om**" as in "**from**")
Red	si daeng / สีแดง	see dang ("**dang**" as in "**dangle**")
Green	si kiao / สีเขียว	see key-ou ("**ou**" as in "**out**")
Brown	si namtan / สีน้ำตาล	see numtun
Blue	si namngun สีน้ำเงิน	see num-ngun ("**ng**" as in "**sung**")
Purple	si muang สีม่วง	see moo-ung
Grey	si tao สีเทา	see tao
Black	si dam สีดำ	see dum
Pink	si chompu สีชมพู	see chompoo

1.	neng หนึ่ง	ner-ng ("**ner**" as in "**nerd**", "**ng**" as in "**song**")
2.	song สอง	song
3.	sam สาม	sum
4.	si สี่	see
5.	ha ห้า	hah
6.	hok หก	hock
7.	jet เจ็ด	jet
8.	pet แปด	pad
9.	gao เก้า	gow
10.	sip สิบ	sip
11.	sip et สิบเอ็ด	sip et
12.	sip song สิบสอง	sip song
13.	sip sam สิบสาม	sip sum
14.	sip si สิบสี่	sip see

15.	sip ha สิบห้า	sip hah
16.	sip hok สิบหก	sip hock
17.	sip jet สิบเจ็ด	sip jet
18.	sip bpet สิบแปด	sip pad
19.	sip gao สิบเก้า	sip gow
20	yi sip ยี่สิบ	yie sip ("**yie**" as in "**yield**")
21.	yi sip et ยี่สิบเอ็ด	yie sip et
22.	yi sip song ยี่สิบสอง	yie sip song
23.	yi sip sam ยี่สิบสาม	yie sip sum
24.	yi sip si ยี่สิบสี่	yie sip see
25.	yi sip ha ยี่สิบห้า	yie sip hah
26.	yi sip hok ยี่สิบหก	yie sip hock
27.	yi sip jet ยี่สิบเจ็ด	yie sip jet
28.	yi sip bpet ยี่สิบแปด	yie sip pad
29.	yi sip gao ยี่สิบเก้า	yie sip gow

30.	sam sip สามสิบ	sum sip
40.	si sip สี่สิบ	see sip
50.	ha sip ห้าสิบ	hah sip
60.	hok sip หกสิบ	hock sip
70.	jet sip เจ็ดสิบ	jet sip
80.	bpet sip แปดสิบ	pad sip
90.	gao sip เก้าสิบ	gow sip
100.	neng roi หนึ่งร้อย	ner-ng roy
101.	roi et ร้อยเอ็ด	roy et
200.	song roi สองร้อย	song roy
300.	sam roi สามร้อย	sum roy
400.	si roi สี่ร้อย	see roy
500.	ha roi ห้าร้อย	hah roy
600.	hok roi หกร้อย	hock roy
700.	jet roi เจ็ดร้อย	jet roy

800.	bpet roi แปดร้อย	pad roy
900.	gao roi เก้าร้อย	gow roy
1000.	neng pan หนึ่งพัน	ner-ng pun
10,000	men หมื่น	mern (**"mer"** as in **mermaid"**)
100,000	sen แสน	san ("san" as in "San Francisco")
1,000,000	lan ล้าน	larn
Less.	noi gwa น้อยกว่า	noy gua
Half.	kreng ครึ่ง	kruhng (**"uh"** as in **"duh"**)
More.	mak gwa มากกว่า	mark gua (without the rolling **"r"** sound)

Directions and Transportation

	Translation	How to say it
North	tit nuea ทิศเหนือ	teet newer (without the "r" sound)
South	tit dtai ทิศใต้	teet tie
West	tit dtawan dtok ทิศตะวันตก	teet ta-one tock
East	tit dtawan ok ทิศตะวันออก	tit ta-one ork ("**ork**" as in "**stork**")
Uphill	ken nen ขึ้นเนิน	kern nern ("**ern**" as in "**kernel**")
Downhill	long nen ลงเนิน	long nern
Left	sai ซ้าย	sie
Right	kwa ขวา	qua
Straight ahead.	dtrong bpai kang na ตรงไปข้างหน้า	trong pie cung na
To the left.	bpai tang sai ไปทางซ้าย	pai tung sie

Turn left.	liaw sai เลี้ยวซ้าย	lee-ou sie
To the right.	bpai tang kwa ไปทางขวา	pie tung qua
Turn right.	liao kwa เลี้ยวขวา	lee-ou kwa
How do I get to...?	chan ja bpai … yang rai ฉันจะไป …. อย่างไร	chun ja pie … young rye
... the bus station?	satani konsong สถานีขนส่ง	sa-tar-nee con song (without the "r" sound)
... the airport?	sanam bin สนามบิน	sa-num bean
... downtown?	dtua mueang ตัวเมือง	tua moo-ung
... the train station?	satani rotfai สถานีรถไฟ?	sa-tar-nee rot fai ("fai" as "fi" in "fire" ; without the "r" sound)
... the youth hostel?	yut hotten ยูธโฮสเทล	youth hostel
... the hotel?	rong rem โรงแรม	rong ram
... the embassy?	satan tut สถานทูต	sa-tarn toot (without the "r" sound)

... the consulate?	satan gongsun สถานกงสุล	sa-tarn gong soon (without the "r" sound)
Where is the bus/train station?	satani konsong / satani rotfai yu nai สถานีขนส่ง/สถานีรถไฟอยู่ไหน?	sa-tarnee con song / sa-tarnee rot fai you nai
Excuse me, I am looking for the ticket office.	kho tot khrap / kha chan gamlang ha ti jamnai dtua ขอโทษ ครับ / ค่ะ ฉัน กำลังหาที่จำหน่ายตั๋ว	caw tot crup / ka, chun gumlung hah tee jum nigh tour (without the "r" sound)
I would like a one way ticket to....	chan dtong gan dtua den tang bpai... ฉันต้องการตั๋วเดินทางไป.....	chun tong gun tour dern tang (without the "r" sounds)
I would like a round trip ticket to....	chan dtong gan dtua den tang rop bpai glap ... ฉันต้องการตั๋วเดินทางรอบไป-กลับ	chun tong gun tua dern tang rob pie glup
I would like to sit in the smoking car.	chan dtong gan nang nai rot sup buri ฉันต้องการที่จะนั่งในรถสูบบุหรี่	chun tong gun nung nai rot soup boo-ree
I would like to sit in the non-smoking car.	chan dtong gan ti ja nang nai rot ham sup buri ฉันต้องการที่จะนั่งในรถห้ามสูบบุหรี่	chun tong gun tee ja nung nai rot harm soup boo-ree

Where does this train/bus go?	rotfai / rotbat an ni bpai nai รถไฟ/รถบัสอันนี้ไปไหน?	rot fai / rot bus un nee pie nai
Where is the train/bus to...?	rotfai/rotbat bpai … yu nai รถไฟ/รถบัสไป...อยู่ไหน?	rot fai / rot bus pie … you nai
Does this train/bus stop in...?	rotfai/rotbat jot ti … mai รถไฟ/รถบัสจอดที่...ไหม	rot fai / rot bus jot tee … mai
What is the departure and arrival time?	ok wela arai le teng wela arai ออกเวลาอะไร และถึงเวลาอะไร?	ork whe-la a-rye le terng whela a-rye
How much is a first class ticket?	dtua chan neng tao rai ตั๋วชั้นหนึ่งเท่าไหร่?	tua chun nerng tao rye
Entrance.	tang kao ทางเข้า	tung cow
Exit.	tang ok ทางออก	tung ork
Where is the bus stop?	bpai rot me yu ti nai ป้ายรถเมล์อยู่ที่ไหน	pai rot mare you tee nai
One way ticket.	dtua tiaw diaw ตั๋วเที่ยวเดียว	tua tee-ou dee-ou
A round trip ticket.	dtua bpai glap ตั๋วไปกลับ	tua pie glup

Do you go to...	khun ja bpai … mai คุณจะไป ... ไหม	coon ja pie … my
Do you have a schedule?	khun mi dtarang wela mai คุณมีตารางเวลาไหม	coon me tarung whe-la my
Which direction do I have to go?	chan dtong bpai tit tang nai ฉันต้องไปทิศทางไหน	chun tong pie teet tung nai
How often do the trains run?	rotfai wing boi kanat nai รถไฟวิ่งบ่อยขนาดไหน	rot fai wing boy canut nai
How many stops are there?	jot gi ti จอดกี่ที่	jot gee tee ("**g**" as in "**go**")
Please tell me when we get there?	garuna bok chan dui muea rao teng lew กรุณาบอกฉันด้วยเมื่อเราถึงแล้ว	garoona bog chun doy, moo-ar rou terng lou ("**lou**" as in "**loud**")
How do I get there?	chan dtong bpai yang ngai ฉันต้องไปยังไง	chun tong pie young ngai
Where is the closest metro station?	satani rotfai dtai din ti glai tisut yu tinai สถานีรถไฟใต้ดินที่ใกล้ที่สุดอยู่ที่ไหน	sa-tarnee rot fai tie-dean tee glai teesoot
How much is the fare?	ka doi san taorai ค่าโดยสารเท่าไหร่	car doy sarn tao rye

How long does it stop?	man ja jot nan kanat nai มันจะจอดนานขนาดไหน	mun ja jot nun canut nai
How long does it stop?	man ja jot nan kanat nai มันจะจอดนานขนาดไหน	mun ja jot nun canut nai
From what platform does it leave?	man ok jak chanchala nai มันออกจากชานชลาไหน	mun ork juck chun chala nai
Do I have to change trains?	chan ja dtong bplian rotfai mai ฉันจะต้องเปลี่ยนรถไฟไหม	chun ja tong plee-un rot fai my
Is this place taken?	ti nang ni wang mai ที่นั่งนี้ว่างไหม	tee nung nee wung my
How much does it cost?	raka tao rai ราคาเท่าไหร่	ra-car tao rai
Where do I get off?	chan tong long ti nai ฉันต้องลงที่ไหน	chun tong long tee nai
What time does the train leave?	rotfai ja ok gi mong รถไฟจะออกกี่โมง?	rot fai ork gui mong ("**gui**" as in "**guitar**")
Towards the...	bpai tang ไปทาง ...	pie tung
Past the...	pan ... ผ่าน ...	pun
Before the...	gon ... ก่อน ...	gone
Street	tanon ถนน	ta-nun

Intersection	si yek สี่แยก	see yack
One way	wan we วันเวย์	one way
No parking	ham jot ห้ามจอด	harm jot
Gas/petrol station	bpam gat / bpam nam man ปั้มก๊าซ / ปั้มน้ำมัน	pump gas / pump num mun
Gas/petrol	gat / nam man ก๊าซ / น้ำมัน	gas / num mun
Diesel	disen ดีเซล	disel
Fare	ka doi san ค่าโดยสาร	ka doy sarn
Speed limit	jam gat kwam rew จำกัดความเร็ว	kum gut kuam row
Taxi!	teksi แท็กซี่	taxi
Take me to...., please.	garuna pa chan bpai … กรุณาพาฉันไป	garoona pa chun pie …
How much does it cost to go to...?	bpai … tao rai ไป...เท่าไร	pie … tao rye
Take me there, please.	garuna pa chan pai non กรุณาพาฉันไปโน้น	garoona pa chun pai norn
Is there a subway in this city?	mi rot fai den nai mueang ni mai มีรถไฟใต้ดินในเมืองนี้ไหม	mee rot fai dern nai moo-ung nee

		my
Where can I buy a ticket?	chan samart sue dtua dai ti nai ฉันสามารถซื้อตั๋วได้ที่ไหน	chun samart sir tour die tee nai (without the "**r**" sounds)
Do you have a map showing the subway stops?	mi penti sadeng jut jot kong rot fai dtai din mai มีแผนที่แสดงจุดจอดของรถไฟใต้ดินไหม	me pantee sa-dang joot jot kong rot fai tai dean mai
Can you show me on the map?	khun chi penti hai chan du dai mai คุณชี้แผนที่ให้ฉันดู ได้ไหม	coon chee pantee hi chun doo die my
Please take me to this address.	garuna pa chan pai ti yu ni กรุณาพาฉันไปที่อยู่นี่	garoona pa chun pie tee you nee
Is it far from here?	man yu glai jak ti ni mai มันอยู่ไกลจากที่นี่ไหม	man you glie juck tee nee mai
I am lost.	chan luang tang ฉันหลงทาง	chuan loo-ung tung
I want to rent a car.	chan dtong gan chao rot ฉันต้องการเช่ารถ	chan tong gun chow rot

Emergencies and Problem Phrases

	Translation	**How to say it**
Help!	chuai dui ช่วยด้วย	choy doy
What is wrong?	bpen arai เป็นอะไร	pen a rye
Leave me alone.	hai chan yu kon diao ให้ฉันอยู่คนเดียว	hi chun you kon dee-ow
Don't touch me!	ya jap chan อย่าจับฉัน	ya jup chun
I will call the police.	chan ja tor riak tamruat ฉันจะโทรเรียกตำรวจ	chun ja tore riak tum ruat
Police!	tamruat ตำรวจ	tum ruat
Stop! Thief!	yut kamoi หยุด ขโมย	yoot! kamoy!
It's an emergency.	man bpen hetgan chukchen มันเป็นเหตุการณ์ฉุกเฉิน	mun pen het gun chook chern
I need help.	chan yak dai kwam chuai luea	chun yuck die quam choy loo-er (without the "**r**" sound)

	ฉันอยากได้ความช่วยเหลือ	
I'm lost.	chan luang tang ฉันหลงทาง	chun loo-ung tung

Medical

	Translation	How to say it
I have pain.	chan jep bpuat ฉันเจ็บปวด	chun jep poo-ut ("**ut**" as in "**hut**"
I have a stomach ache.	chan bpuat tong ฉันปวดท้อง	chun poo-ut tong
I am a diabetic.	chan bpen rok bao wan ฉันเป็นโรคเบาหวาน	chan pen rock bou one (long "**o**" in "**rock**" ; "**ou**" as in "**out**")
I have backache.	chan bpuat lang ฉันปวดหลัง	chun poo-ut lung
I have a toothache.	chan bpuan fan ฉันปวดฟัน	chun poo-ut fun
I do not feel good.	chan rusuk mai di ฉันรู้สึกไม่ดี	chun roo-serk my dee ("**erk**" as in "**perk**" but without an "**r**" sound)
I have chest-pain.	chan nen na-ok ฉันแน่นหน้าอก	chun nan na-ork ("without an "**r**" sound)
I had a heart attack.	hua jai wai หัวใจวาย	hoo-ha jie why
I have cramps.	bpen dtakhiw เป็นตะคิว	pen ta cue
I have a sore throat.	chan jep kho ฉันเจ็บคอ	chun jep core

		(without the "**r**" sound)
I am allergic to…	chan pe… ฉันแพ้...	chun pare (without the "**r**" sound)
I need a doctor.	chan dtonggan pop mo ฉันต้องการพบหมอ	chan tong gun pop more (without the "**r**" sound)
I need a dentist.	chan dtonggan pop mo fan ฉันต้องการพบหมอฟัน	chan tong gun pop more fun (without the "**r**" sound)
I need a nurse.	chan dtonggan nang payaban ฉันต้องการนางพยาบาล	chan tong gun nung pie-a-barn (without the "**r**" sound)
I feel sick.	chan rusuk bpuai ฉันรู้สึกป่วย	chun roo-serk poo-eye ("**erk**" as in "**perk**" but without an "**r**" sound)
I have a headache.	chan bpuat hua ฉันปวดหัว	chuan poo-ut hoo-a
I think that I have the flu.	chan kit wa chan bpen kai wat ฉันคิดว่าฉันเป็นไข้หวัด	chun kit wa chun pen kai what ("**wa**" as in "**wash**")
I feel dizzy.	chan rusuk men hua ฉันรู้สึกมึนหัว	chun roo-serk mern hoo-a
I feel nauseous.	chan ajian ฉันอาเจียน	chun a-jee-un
I have fever.	chan pen kai ฉันเป็นไข้	chun pen kai

It hurts here.	man jep ti ni มันเจ็บที่นี่	mun jep tee nee
Where's a hospital?	rong payaban yu ti nai โรงพยาบาลอยู่ที่ไหน	rong pie-a-barn you tee nai (without the "**r**" sound)

Money

	Translation	How to say it
Do you accept American dollars?	khun rab ngun donla saharat mai คุณรับเงินดอลล่าสหรัฐไหม	coon rup ngun Dollar saharut my
Do you accept Euros?	khun rab ngun yuro mai คุณรับเงินยูโรไหม	coon rup ngun Euro my
Do you accept British pounds?	khun rab ngun bpon mai คุณรับเงินปอนด์ไหม	coon rup ngun Pound my
Do you accept credit cards?	khun rap bat kredit mai คุณรับบัตรเครดิตไหม	coon rup but credit my
Where can I find an ATM?	mi e ti em yu ti nai มีเอทีเอ็มอยู่ที่ไหน	me ATM you tee nai
Where can I withdraw money?	chan ton ngun dai ti nai ฉันถอนเงินได้ที่ไหน	chun torn ngun die tee nai
Where is the bank?	tanakhan yu ti nai ธนาคารอยู่ที่ไหน	tannakarn you tee nai (without the "r" sound)
What is the exchange rate?	atara lek bplian tao rai อัตราแลกเปลี่ยนเท่าใด	uttera lek plian tao rye
Where can I get money changed?	chan lek bplian ngun dai ti nai ฉันแลกเปลี่ยนเงินได้ที่ไหน	chun lek plian ngun die tee nai
Can you change	khun lek bplian ngun hai chan	coon lep plian

money for me?	dai mai คุณแลกเปลี่ยนเงินให้ฉันได้ไหม	ngun hi chun dai my
Where can I get a traveler's check changed?	chan lek bplian chek den tang dai ti nai ฉันแลกเปลี่ยนเช็คเดินทางได้ที่ไหน	chun lek plain check dern tung die tee nai
Can you change a traveler's check for me?	khun lek bplian chek den tang hai chan dai mai คุณแลกเปลี่ยนเช็คเดินทางให้ฉันได้ไหม	coon lek plian check dern tang hi chun die my

Shopping

	Translation	How to say it
I am looking for a shopping center.	ฉันกำลังหาศูนย์การค้า chan gamlang ha sun ganka	chun gum lung hah soon gun car (without the "**r**" sound)
Where can I find a department store?	ฉันสามารถหาห้างสรรพสินค้าได้ที่ไหน chan samart ha hang sapasinka dai ti nai	chun sa-mart hah hung sappa-sinka die tee nai
Where can I find a gift shop?	ฉันสามารถหาร้านกิ๊ฟช๊อปได้ที่ไหน chan samart ha ran gipshop dai ti nai	chun sa-mart hah run gift shop die tee nai
Where can I find a market?	ฉันสามารถหาตลาดได้ที่ไหน chan samart ha dtalat dai ti nai	chun sa-mart hah ta-lart die tee nai
Where can I find a clothing store?	ฉันสามารถหาร้านขายเสื้อผ้าได้ที่ไหน chan samart ha ran kai sueapa dai ti nai	chun sa-mart hah run kai soo-er pa die tee nai ("**er**" as in "**water**" ; "**pa**" as in "**part**"
Please show me.	กรุณาให้ฉันดู garuna hai chan du	garoona hi chun doo

I'd like something.	ฉันอยากจะได้สิ่งที่... chan yak ja dai sing ti …	chun yuck ja die sing tee
I need...	ฉันต้องการ... chan dtong gan …	chan tong gun …
... batteries	ถ่าน tan	tarn (without the "**r**" sound)
… a pen	ปากกา bpakga	Parker
... condoms	ถุงยางอนามัย tung ya anamai	toong ya a-na-my ("**ya**" as in "**yard**")
… change	เงินทอน ngun ton	ngun torn
… a postcard	โปสการ์ด bposgat	postcard
… postage stamps	แสตมป์ satem	stamp
… a razor	...มีดโกน …mitgon	meet gone
… shampoo	...แชมพู …chempu	shampoo
…aspirin	แอสไพริน espairin	aspirin
... cold medicine	...ยาสำหรับเป็นหวัด …yasamrap bpen wat	ya sumrup pen what
... stomach medicine	ยาสำหรับปวดท้อง ya samrap bpuat tong	ya sumrup poo-ut tong
... soap	สบู่ sobu	so-boo
... tampons	สำลีอนามัย samli anamai	sumlee a-na-

		my
... writing paper	กระดาษเขียน gradat kian	gra-dut kian
... sunblock lotion	ครีมกันแดด krim gan det	cream gun dat ("**at**" as in "**hat**")
... toothpaste	ยาสีฟัน ya si fan	ya see fun
... a toothbrush	แปรงสีฟัน bpreng si fan	prang see fun
... an umbrella	ร่ม rom	rom
... English-language books	หนังสือภาษาอังกฤษ nangsue pasa angrit	nungser passa ungreet
... English-language magazines	นิตยสารภาษาอังกฤษ nitayasan pasa angrit	neat-a-ya-sun passa ungreet
... English-language newspaper	หนังสือพิมพ์ภาษาอังกฤษ nangsue pim pasa angrit	nungser pim passa ungreet
Do you take VISA?	คุณรับบัตรวีซ่าไหม kun rap bat wisa mai	coon rup but VISA my
Do you take debit cards?	คุณรับบัตรเดบิตไหม kun rap bat debit mai	coon rup but debit my
Do you take American dollars?	คุณรับเงินสหรัฐไหม kun rap ngun saharat mai	coon rup ngun saharut my
Do you have?	มี...ไหม mi...mai	me ... my
Do you have	มีอันนี้ที่เป็นไซด์ของฉันไหม mi an ni	me un nee pen

this in my size?	bpen sai kong chan mai	size kong chun my
Expensive	แพง peng	pang
Cheap	ถูก tuk	took
I'd like to try it on.	ฉันอยากจะสวมลองดู chan yak ja suam long du	chun yuck ja soo-um long doo
It does not fit (me).	ฉันใส่ไม่ได้ chan sai mai dai	chun sie my die
It fits very well.	ใส่ได้ดี sai dai di	sie die dee
How much is it?	มันราคาเท่าไหร่ man raka tao rai	mun ruckar tao rye (**"ruckar"** without the **"r"** ending sound)
I can't afford it.	ฉันไม่มีเงินพอ chan mai mi ngun po	chun my me ngun pore (**"pore"** without the **"re"** sound)
That is too expensive.	มันแพงเกินไป man peng gen bpai	mun pang gern pie
You're cheating me.	คุณโกงฉัน khun gong chan	coon gong chun
I'd like something else.	ฉันอยากจะได้อันอื่น chan yak ja dai an en	chun yuck ja die un earn
I'm not	ฉันไม่สนใจ chan mai sonjai	chun my son jie

interested.		
I don't want it.	ฉันไม่เอามัน chan mai ao man	chun mai ou mun
I will take it.	ฉันจะเอามัน chan ja ao man	chan ja ou mun
Can I have a bag?	ขอถุงหน่อย kho tung noi	caw toong noy
Can you ship it to my country?	คุณจะส่งทางเรือไปประเทศของฉันได้ไหม khun ja song tang ruea bpai bpratet kong chan dai mai	coon ja song tung roo-a pie pratet kong chun die my

Time and Date

	Translation	How to say it
Minute / Minutes	นาที nati	nutty
Hour / Hours	ชั่วโมง chuamong	chew-a-mong
Day / Days	วัน wan	one
Week / Weeks	สัปดาห์ sapda	sup-da ("da" as in "dark")
Month / Months	เดือน duean	dew-un
Year / Years	ปี bpi	pee
3 o'clock AM	ตีสาม dti sam	tee sum
8 o'clock AM	แปดโมงเช้า bpet mong chao	pad mong chow
2 o'clock PM	บ่ายสองโมง bai song mong	bye song mong
9 o'clock PM	สามทุ่ม sam tum	sum toom

Monday	วันจันทร์ wan jan	one jun
Tuesday	วันอังคาร wan angkan	one ung-carn (without the "**r**" sound)
Wednesday	วันพุธ wan put	one put
Thursday	วันพฤหัสบดี wan paruhatsabadi	wan paroo-hut / wan paroo-hut supper-dee (without the "**r**" sound)
Friday	วันศุกร์ wan suk	one sook
Saturday	วันเสาร์ wan sao	one sow
Sunday	วันอาทิตย์ wan atit	one a-teet
Today	วันนี้ wan ni	one nee
Yesterday	เมื่อวาน muea wan	moo-a one
Tomorrow	พรุ่งนี้ prung ni	proong nee
This Week	สัปดาห์นี้ sapda ni	sup-da nee
Last Week	สัปดาห์ที่แล้ว sapda ti lew	sup-da tee lou ("**lou**" as in "**loud**")

Next Week	สัปดาห์หน้า sapda na	sup-da na ("**a**" as in "**after**")
January	มกราคม mokgarakom	mocker-a-com
February	กุมภาพันธ์ gumpapan	goom-pa-pun
March	มีนาคม minakom	me-na-com
April	เมษายน mesayon	me-sa-yon
May	พฤษภาคม prutsapakom	proot-sa-pa-com
June	มิถุนายน mitunayon	me-tuna-yon
July	กรกฎาคม garagadakom	garaka-da-com
August	สิงหาคม singhakom	sing-hah-com
September	กันยายน ganyayon	gun-ya-yon
October	ตุลาคม dtulakom	tool-a-com
November	พฤศจิกายน	proot-sa-jee-ga-yon

	prutsajigayon	
December	ธันวาคม tanwakom	tun-wha-com
June 13th, 2003	สิบสาม มิถุนายน ปีสองพันสาม sip sam mitunakom bpi song pan sam	sip sum me-tuna-com pee song pun sum
October 21st, 1999	ยี่สิบเอ็ด ตุลาคม ปีหนึ่งพันเก้าร้อยเก้าสิบเก้า yisip et dtulakom bpi neng pan gao roi gao sip gao	yee-sip et tool-a-com pee ner-ng pun

Made in the USA
Las Vegas, NV
07 January 2025

15968679R00033